iScience
Readers

Sun, Moon, and Stars:
A Cosmic Case

by Emily Sohn and Adam Harter

Chief Content Consultant
Edward Rock
Associate Executive Director, National Science Teachers Association

NORWOODHOUSE PRESS
Chicago, Illinois

Norwood House Press
PO Box 316598
Chicago, IL 60631

For information regarding Norwood House Press, please visit our website at
www.norwoodhousepress.com or call 866-565-2900.

Special thanks to: Amanda Jones, Amy Karasick, Alanna Mertens, Terrence Young, Jr.

Editor: Barbara J. Foster
Designer: Daniel M. Greene
Production Management: Victory Productions, Inc.

This book was manufactured as a paperback edition. If you are purchasing this book as a rebound
hardcover or without any cover, the publisher and any licensors' rights are being violated.

Paperback ISBN: 978-1-60357-287-3

The Library of Congress has cataloged the original hardcover edition with the following
call number: 2010044537

© 2011 by Norwood House Press. All Rights Reserved. No part of this book may be reproduced
without written permission from the publisher.

282R—082015
Printed in ShenZhen, Guangdong, China.

CONTENTS

Note to Caregivers:

Throughout this book, many questions are posed to the reader. Some are open-ended and ask what the reader thinks. Discuss these questions with your child and guide him or her in thinking through the possible answers and outcomes. There are also questions posed which have a specific answer. Encourage your child to read through the text to determine the correct answer. Most importantly, encourage answers grounded in reality while also allowing imaginations to soar. Information to help support you as you share the book with your child is provided in the back in the **Additional Notes** section.

Words that are **bolded** are defined in the glossary in the back of the book.

It's No Great Mystery!

It happens every day and every night. The **Sun, Moon,** and **stars** move across the sky. People have long watched these objects with wonder. What are they? Why do they keep moving? In this book, you will learn about the objects that appear to move in regular patterns across the sky. You will also be a detective. You will be able to use what you learn about the Sun, Moon, and stars to solve a mystery.

A Cosmic Whodunit

An Ohio bank was robbed at 4:30 one winter afternoon. The police have four suspects. They asked each suspect where he or she was at 4:30. As you read this book, you will find clues to help you figure out who is not telling the truth.

Where were you at 4:30?

Suspect 1: Diz Aster

"I was reading in the library. The Sun was shining low through a window facing west. It was bright. So, I had to close the shades."

Suspect 2: May Hem

"I was taking a nap in the hotel. I was tired because I had been up all night with a headache. Every few hours last night, I went to the roof for some air. Up there, I saw a star above the bank. Each time I looked, the star was in the same place."

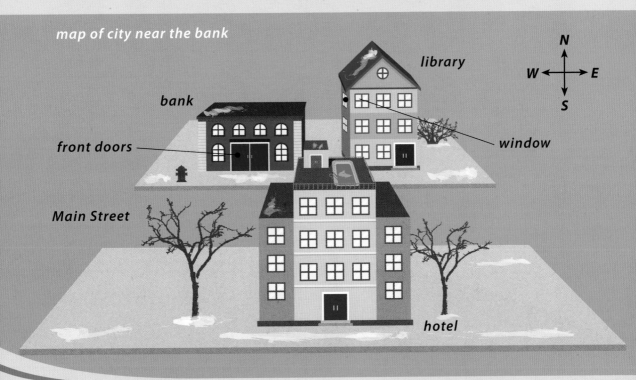

map of city near the bank

Suspect 3: Troy Bell

"I was outside the hotel. I saw Dee Seat come out of the bank. It was late in the afternoon. The Sun was low in the sky. I remember that Dee Seat had a short **shadow.** She must be the robber!"

Suspect 4: Dee Seat

"Sure, I was at the bank. But I didn't steal any money. As I left the bank, I saw the crescent moon near the setting Sun. Its shape reminded me to buy bananas."

Do you know who stole the money? No? Try the Discover Activity to get started. Then, keep reading. You will learn about the Sun, Moon, and stars. Along the way, you will find clues that will help you solve the crime.

softball

Model the Moon

Knowing how the Sun shines on the Moon on different days may help you solve the mystery. Grab a lamp and set it up on a table as shown on the next page. Turn it on. Turn off all other lights in the room and close any shades or blinds.

gooseneck lamp

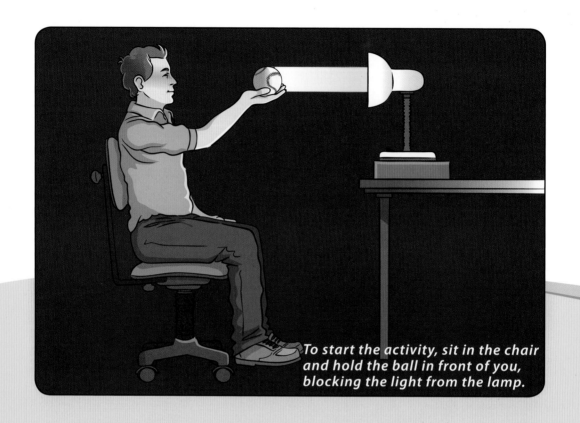

To start the activity, sit in the chair and hold the ball in front of you, blocking the light from the lamp.

Sit in the swivel chair. Hold the ball in your palm. Sit facing the light. Hold the ball up so that it blocks all the light. Now, keep holding the ball at that level. Slowly turn left in the chair until you have made a complete circle. Watch the light on the ball as you turn.

Imagine that the ball is the Moon and the light is the Sun. What do you see? How does the Sun's light change on the Moon as you turn in the chair?

The lighted area on the ball changes shape as you move around in the chair. Exactly how the ball looks depends on where the ball is compared to the light. In a similar way, the Moon's shape appears to change as it moves around Earth. Why? Because we see different parts of the lit half of the Moon as the Moon goes around Earth.

From left to right: the Moon, Earth, and Sun in space

To solve the bank mystery, you will need to see how objects in the sky move. You will also need to know why they look the way they do. Go outside today, tonight, and tomorrow. As the days and nights pass, watch the Sun, Moon, and stars. Take notes. What you see may help you solve the puzzle.

How Does the Moon Move Through Space?

The Moon may look lazy and slow. But it is always moving. A moon **orbits** a planet. Some planets, such as Venus, have no moons. Other planets have many moons. Jupiter has 63 moons. Earth has just one moon.

The Moon orbits Earth.

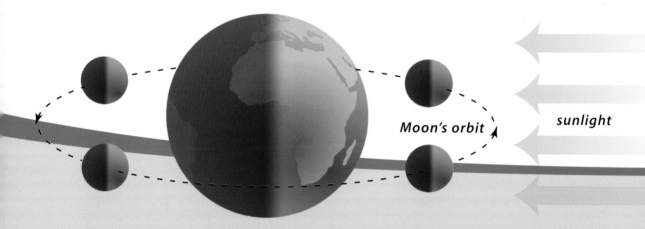

Moon's orbit

sunlight

Shape-Shifter

If you like looking at the Moon, thank the Sun. Sunlight bounces off the Moon and back to our eyes. That's what lets us see it. The same side of the Moon always faces Earth. That's the side we see. As the Moon orbits Earth, it appears in different shapes. It can be big and round or shaped like a curved sliver. These shapes are called **phases.**

On the darkest nights, there seems to be no Moon at all. This phase is called a new moon. It happens when the Moon is between Earth and the Sun. Sunlight is shining on the back of the Moon, so we can't see the front. A few days later, a slim piece of the Moon shows up. This phase is a crescent moon. It gets bigger every night. Now, you can see only the right side of the Moon. When you can see more than half of the Moon, you see a gibbous moon. Later, you can see the whole round face of the lit side. This phase is the full moon.

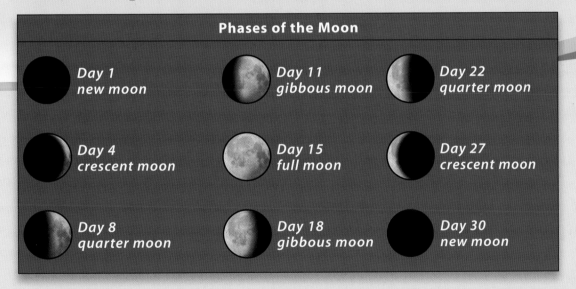

Phases of the Moon

Day 1
new moon

Day 11
gibbous moon

Day 22
quarter moon

Day 4
crescent moon

Day 15
full moon

Day 27
crescent moon

Day 8
quarter moon

Day 18
gibbous moon

Day 30
new moon

For two weeks after the full moon, you see only part of the Moon again. Then, you can see just the left side. The cycle takes about 29 days. Finally, there is another new moon.

Hello Moon, Where Are You?

The Moon can seem like a bunny in a magic show. Some nights, it's there. Other nights, it seems to be gone. But the Moon follows a pattern. It rises and sets each day, just like the Sun. Also like the Sun, it rises in the east and sets in the west. But it rises and sets at different times on different days. The exact times depend on what phase it's in.

moonrise over a desert

The Moon goes around Earth once every month. As Earth travels, it also spins like a top. Go back into the room with the ball, the chair, and the lamp. You are the Earth. The ball is the Moon. How can you show the spinning of the Earth? How can you show the Moon's orbit? Could having a partner help?

14

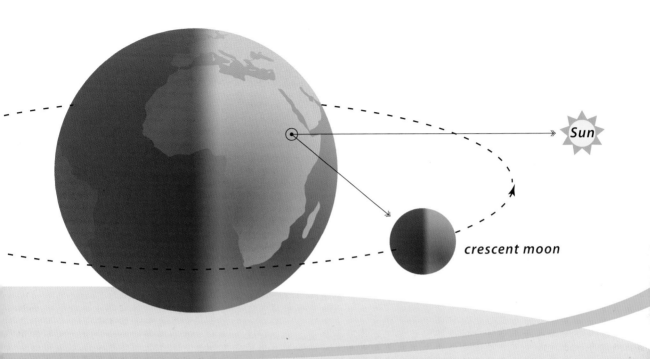

Sun

crescent moon

Remember Dee Seat's answer in the whodunit? She said she saw the crescent moon near the Sun. Can you ever see the Moon during the daytime? At 4:30, where do you think you would see the crescent moon compared to the Sun? To find out, go back to your lamp model. Hold the ball in the light where it looks like a crescent. Is the Moon close to the Sun? Or is it far away? Do you think Dee Seat is telling the truth?

How Can You Model Earth and the Sun?

The Sun rises in the east over these trees.

How Does the Sun Move Across the Sky?

Day after day, the Sun rises in the east and sets in the west. Have a friend pretend to be the Sun. You are the Earth. See if you can make the Sun rise and set in your model. Can you think of two ways to do this?

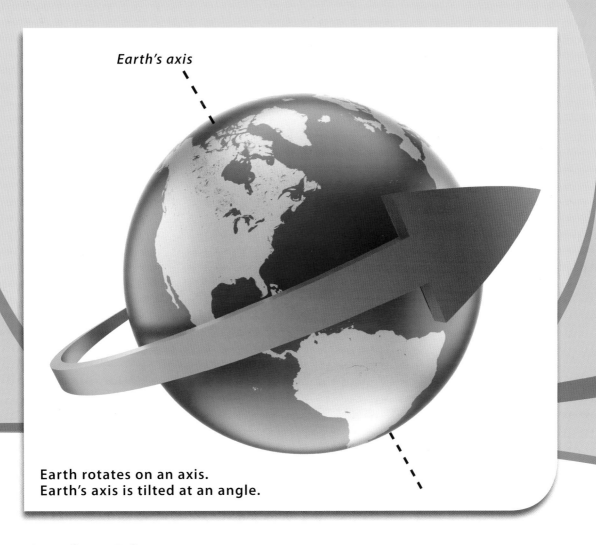

Earth's axis

Earth rotates on an axis.
Earth's axis is tilted at an angle.

Getting Dizzy

It takes a whole month for the Moon to orbit Earth. So why can you see the Moon move across the sky in a single night? Because Earth spins on an imaginary line called its **axis.** One complete spin takes one day. As our world turns, objects in space look like they're moving. Earth's motion explains why the Sun appears to rise and set every day.

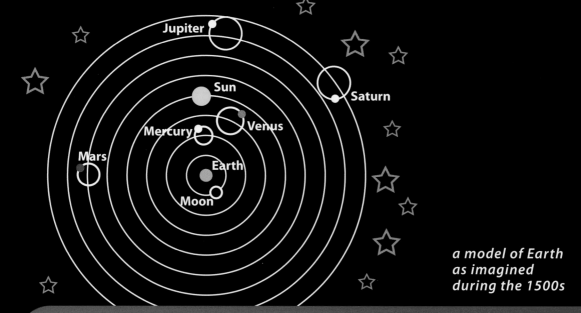

a model of Earth as imagined during the 1500s

Connecting to History

Galileo Galilei

Hundreds of years ago, most people believed that Earth was the center of the **universe.** They thought the Sun moved around Earth. To them, that explained the Sun's path across the sky.

Then came Galileo Galilei (1564–1642). One hundred years before, Nicolaus Copernicus had put forth the revolutionary idea that Earth revolved around the Sun. Galileo was one of the first scientists to support this idea. When Galileo looked through a **telescope,** he saw moons orbiting Jupiter. He realized that Earth was not at the center of the universe.

Galileo tried to convince people that Earth moved around the Sun. But it took the work of many scientists several hundred years to change everyone's views.

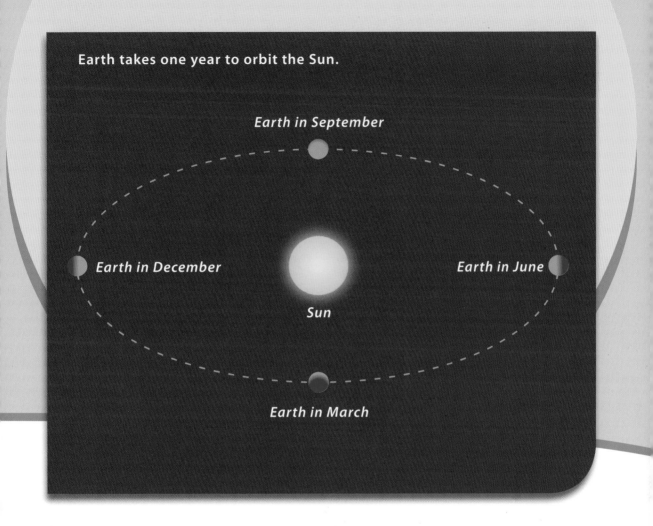

Earth takes one year to orbit the Sun.

Earth in September

Earth in December

Sun

Earth in June

Earth in March

Hot Center

The Sun plays tricks on our eyes every day. It looks like it's going around us. But the opposite is true! Earth and seven other planets orbit the Sun. It takes Earth one year to make one loop around the Sun.

Sun Tracks

The Sun is too big to get lost. But it can really keep you guessing. Imagine going to a hot country on the **equator,** such as Ecuador. As the day begins, the Sun rises in the east. It reaches its highest point at noon. At that hour, it is overhead. Then, it sinks again and sets in the west.

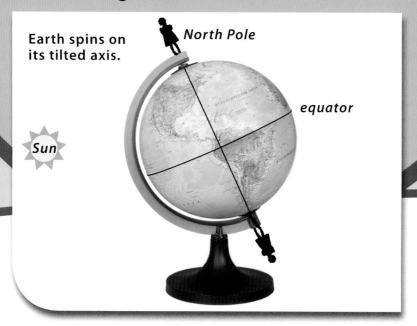

Earth spins on its tilted axis.

North Pole

equator

Sun

Now, imagine you have traveled to the North Pole. You have arrived at the beginning of summer. The Earth is tilted at an angle. So now, the North Pole points toward the Sun. As Earth spins, the Sun seems to move around and around in the sky. It does not get lower or higher. In the summer there, daytime never ends! During the winter at the North Pole, the Sun never rises. It is dark all the time!

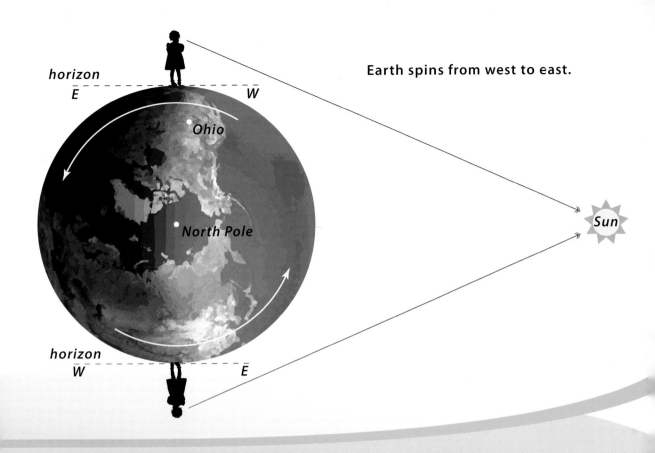

horizon

E   W

Ohio

North Pole

horizon

W   E

Earth spins from west to east.

Sun

Keep traveling. Imagine you are now in the Southern Hemisphere. This is the area south of the equator. Even at noon here, the Sun is in the northern part of the sky.

Take one more imaginary trip. This time you land in Ohio. Where would the Sun be at 4:30 p.m. in winter? No matter where you are, when the Sun rises, it rises in the east. When the Sun sets, it sets in the west.

Suspect Diz Aster said that the Sun was shining in through a window that faced west. Do you think she was telling the truth?

Shadowy Secrets

Shadows sometimes scare dogs and small children. But shadows can tell you a lot about the Sun. A shadow forms when an object blocks sunlight. Shadows are long early in the morning and late in the afternoon. At those times, the Sun is low in the sky.

Shadows are longest in the early morning and just before sunset.

When the Sun is higher, shadows are shorter. At what time of day do you think your shadow would be shortest? Do you think shadows are shorter in some parts of the world than in others?

Suspect Troy Bell said that Dee had a short shadow when she came out of the bank. Do you think he was telling the truth?

Science at Work

Photographer

Click! When you take a picture, you should point your camera away from the Sun. Sunlight "tricks" the camera. If you point your camera right at the Sun, the camera lets in less light. Your photo will be too dark.

Think about what time it is and where the Sun is when you want to take a photograph. That can help you play with shadows. Photographers use shadows to make pictures more interesting. Go outside and look at shadows. Can you frame a good picture with your fingers? Or better yet, if you have a real camera, try it that way!

Photographers use light to create images.

the Sun, Earth, and the Moon lined up in space

What Is a Star?

Some objects, such as the Moon, reflect light. Other objects, such as stars, make their own light. Stars shine by smashing together atoms (tiny pieces) of hydrogen. Hydrogen is a gas. It makes up the center, or core, of a star. When hydrogen atoms slam together, they release huge amounts of energy. We see some of that energy as light.

The most famous star is the Sun. The Sun is the closest star to Earth. It is 93 million miles away from Earth. It is not the biggest or the brightest star in space. It just looks that way because it's so close to us.

Some stars are brighter than others. But you can't tell on your own which outshine the rest. If you look at night, you will be fooled by the closest stars. Other stars appear dim because they are so far away.

the Big Dipper

Star Parties

Do you ever see shapes and pictures in the stars? **Constellations** are groups of stars that form patterns. One popular example is the Big Dipper. What common object does the Big Dipper look like?

Always Moving

The Sun and the Moon aren't the only objects that move through the sky. Stars rise in the east and set in the west, too. The stars seem to move for the same reason the Sun does. As the Earth spins, we're the ones who are really moving.

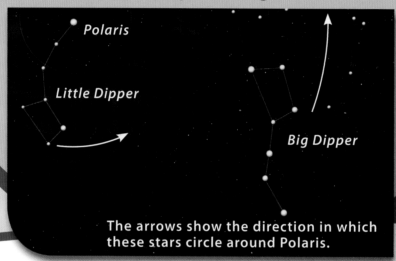

The arrows show the direction in which these stars circle around Polaris.

But, one star does not move. It is called **Polaris,** or the North Star. If you stayed up all night long, you would see all the stars slowly moving around it. The North Star stays put because Earth's axis points right at it. Long ago, sailors used Polaris to find their way at sea. Polaris is part of a constellation called the Little Dipper. It is at the end of the dipper's handle.

Suspect May Hem said she saw a star above the bank that did not move. Do you think she was telling the truth?